P. & O. Pencillings

By W·W·Lloyd·

QUIS SEPARABIT

GOING ON BOARD AT TILBURY.

IN THE RIVER.

THE PILOT LEAVING THE SHIP OFF THE ISLE OF WIGHT.

PUBLISHED FOR

The Peninsular and Oriental Steam Navigation Company,

122, LEADENHALL STREET, LONDON, E.C.

BY

Day & Son, 21a, Berners Street London W.

Sea Reach

In the Docks

The tug hauling us clear of the jetty

Down the river
Tight navigation

IN THE THAMES

P. & O. PENCILLINGS.

2. THE FIRST DINNER. NOT QUITE SO HUNGRY AS HE THOUGHT HE WAS.

1. BOUND FOR BOMBAY UNDER THE CAPTAIN'S CHARGE, AND OF HIS MANY RESPONSIBILITIES THE HEAVIEST.

4. A PERILOUS JOURNEY.

3. JONES IS NEVER SEASICK, BUT EXPLAINS THAT HE IS SLIGHTLY UPSET BY HIS EARLY BREAKFAST IN TOWN.

6. A LAST GLANCE OF OLD ENGLAND.

5. SMITH FEELS HE MIGHT POSSIBLY SURVIVE ANOTHER TEN MINUTES IF HIS CHARMING COMPANION AND THE ATTENTIVE STEWARDS WOULD LEAVE HIM ALONE.

DOWN CHANNEL

Interior of carriage

Nap

The P&O Brindisi Express. Victoria Station.

Forty winks

THE P. & O. BRINDISI EXPRESS.

1."I'LL CLING TO THEE " (CHRISTY MINSTREL AIR).   KATE ALLENEY DIDN'T HEAR THE LAST FOR A LONG WHILE, OF HER
PECULIAR, THOUGH QUITE UNINTENTIONAL, WAY OF STRIKING AN ACQUAINTANCE WITH JIM DALY OF THE BUFFS.

2. ESPECIALLY FROM HER SISTER, WHO HAD MADE SEVERAL FRIENDS
IN THE ORTHODOX FASHION.

INTRODUCTIONS ORTHODOX AND OTHERWISE

CHAIR HUNTING.

1. SHAVING BEGINS TO BE A SERVICE OF DANGER.

2. AND HAIRDRESSING A MATTER OF SOME DIFFICULTY.

3. WHILE THE RESULT IN BOTH CASES IS HARDLY SATISFACTORY.

OFF USHANT

This is not King John signing the Magna Charta but our Purser telling off the seats for first and second dinner and investigating the demand for side tables

Engine room Visitors

Shaft tunnel

Washing up Time off Ushant
A Compote à la Saloon Steward

Jan 9th A last goodbye at the Dock gates 25° in the shade

Jan 13th In the straits of Gibraltar 65° in the shade

ON DECK AND BELOW.

P. & O. PENCILLINGS.

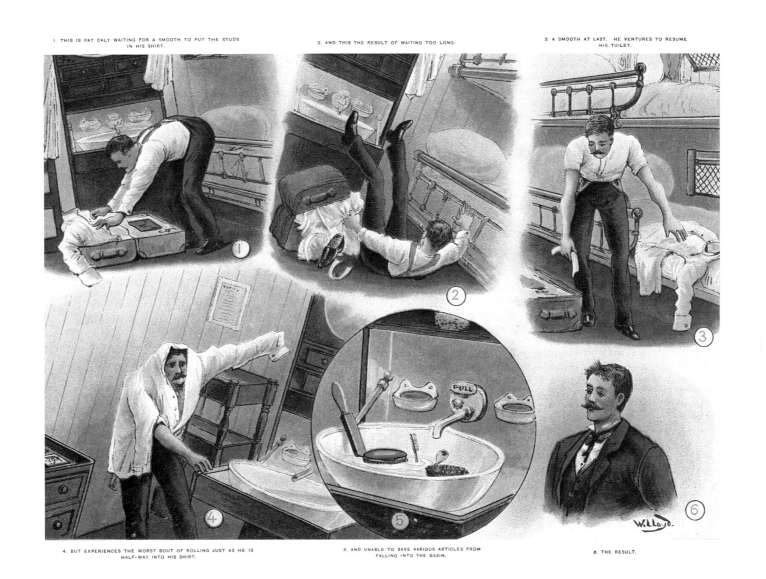

1. THIS IS PAT DALY WAITING FOR A SMOOTH TO PUT THE STUDS IN HIS SHIRT.

2. AND THIS THE RESULT OF WAITING TOO LONG.

3. A SMOOTH AT LAST. HE VENTURES TO RESUME HIS TOILET.

4. BUT EXPERIENCES THE WORST BOUT OF ROLLING JUST AS HE IS HALF-WAY INTO HIS SHIRT.

5. AND UNABLE TO SAVE VARIOUS ARTICLES FROM FALLING INTO THE BASIN.

6. THE RESULT.

IN THE BAY.—DRESSING FOR DINNER.

P. & O. PENCILLINGS.

The Ananias of the Smoking room

The young man Globe Trotting at his parent's expense

The victim of mal de mer who lives on smelling salts

One of our Flirts

The Missionary going to China

The Subaltern returning from leave

A Naval Officer

Thumb nail sketch of the Commander

For Melbourne

Quiet but dangerous

A successful Colonist.

Two little New Zealanders

A Yankee Wanderer (our pianist)

The man who talks a great deal of yachting shop & collapses at the first breeze of wind

Our Foghorns (automatic)

The least troublesome passenger in the ship

Two of the Captain's Wards

The Schoolboy who makes it hot for the gulls with a catapult.

A grass Widdy

A West ender bound for Shepheard's & the Nile

SOME OF THE PASSENGERS.

DINNER TIME.—A WESTERN OCEAN SWELL.

IN THE BAY.

SOME 'BOARD-SHIP HINTS.

P. & O. Pencillings.

1. OFF FOR A RUN ASHORE.

2. THE MEDITERRANEAN ROAD

3. ON THE WESTERN SLOPES. TAKING IT EASY.   5. A BIT OF THE ROCK.   4. NEARLY LEFT BEHIND.

GIBRALTAR.

P. & O. PENCILLINGS.

Off Cape Bon. On deck.

Breakfast rolls.

A corner of our cabin

Afternoon tea on deck.

OFF CAPE BON.

1. A LACE SELLER.

2. FRUIT AND BIRD SELLERS.

MALTA.

Mooring &
Unmooring ship
Signalling the
propeller clear of
steel hawser

The Pilot.

A Maltese "Diso".
Rival boatmen

The English Mail
the P&O boat from Brindisi.

"How much?"
"For you Madam
only twenty shillings"
Five minutes before the Ship starts
"Take it, for seven shillings"!!

MALTA.

"HEAVE FOR A DIVE."

MALTA.

The old style of port

A job after his own heart

A sketch on the "Mirzapore"

A modern P & O port

A cup of comfort 7 a m

A sudden fall in rice

COMFORT AND DISCOMFORT.

P. & O. PENCILLINGS.

A SUNNY BIT OF THE HURRICANE DECK

MEDITERRANEAN WEATHER

A game of Cricket. (tip & run)
A boundary hit.

CRICKET

P. & O. PENCILLINGS.

1. THE OBSTACLE RACE.—THE WATER JUMP.

2. THE BARRELS.—OUR FRIEND THE MAJOR, WHO IS NOT SO THIN AS HE WAS, IS FAIRLY PUZZLED.

3. COCK-FIGHTING.

4. A SCORE FOR BLUE.

SPORTS; OR, A P. & O. RACE MEETING.

Toothache!

Chips and his bench

The Butcher's shop

Forge

'BOARD-SHIP SHOPS.

AN AFTERNOON BASK IN THE SUN.

WARM WEATHER.

The Barber's Shop.

A Bathroom Study.

THE TOILET

P. & O. PENCILLINGS.

OUTWARD BOUND P. & O. MAIL STEAMER ENTERING THE SUEZ CANAL

PORT SAID.

Breakfast,
Tiffin & Dinner bugle
A sketch on the "Arcadia"

A little music
Music-room & Companion "Britannia"

W.

MUSIC.

PASSING THE HOMEWARD BOUND P. & O. "VICTORIA" AT CHALOUF.

IN THE CANAL.

MORE BOARD-SHIP HINTS

P. & O. PENCILLINGS.

THE TOWN OF SUEZ AND THE DOCKS FROM THE CANAL.

IN THE CANAL.

Sunday morning
The Captain reading
Divine Service.

A break in the clouds
Trying to get
a Sight

"The Commander is enjoined to show at all times
the utmost courtesy and attention to passengers"
Extract from Regulations
This is our Skipper endeavouring to carry out
this arduous duty

On the Suez Canal
Arab boys following the P&O Steamer for bucksheesh.

SOME OF THE CAPTAIN'S DUTIES   ARAB BOYS.

P. & O. PENCILLINGS.

1. THE ONLY COOL PLACE IN THE SHIP IS THE REFRIGERATOR, FROM WHICH ON CERTAIN DAYS A STRING OF COOKS AND HELPERS STAGGER BENEATH LOADS OF MEAT FROZEN AS HARD AS IRON, AND DUCKS AND GEESE OF THE CONSISTENCY OF CAST STEEL.

2. WHILE ON SUCH OCCASIONS VISITORS ARE ALLOWED A BRIEF INSPECTION OF THE ICY COLD BLACK HOLE STOCKED WITH MEAT, AND WITH, PERHAPS, A HEAP OF SNOW IN THE CORNER.

3. THE GULF OF SUEZ AND THE RANGE OF JEB EL ATTAKA.

IN THE RED SEA.

The Smoking room

On his way there

THE SMOKING ROOM.

"SEEDIE BOYS" FIREMEN AT WORK.

THE STOKEHOLE.

Breakfast rolls

The Dispensary

Lascars stowing canvas

MORE 'BOARD-SHIP SHOPS.   LASCARS STOWING CANVAS.

P. & O. PENCILLINGS.

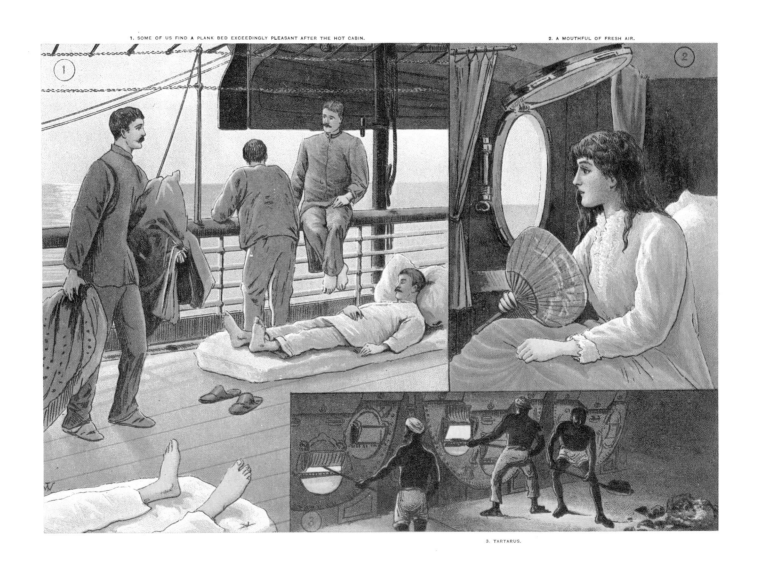

1. SOME OF US FIND A PLANK BED EXCEEDINGLY PLEASANT AFTER THE HOT CABIN.

2. A MOUTHFUL OF FRESH AIR.

3. TARTARUS.

IN THE RED SEA.—A HOT NIGHT.

A Sketch on the Hurricane Deck.

ON DECK.

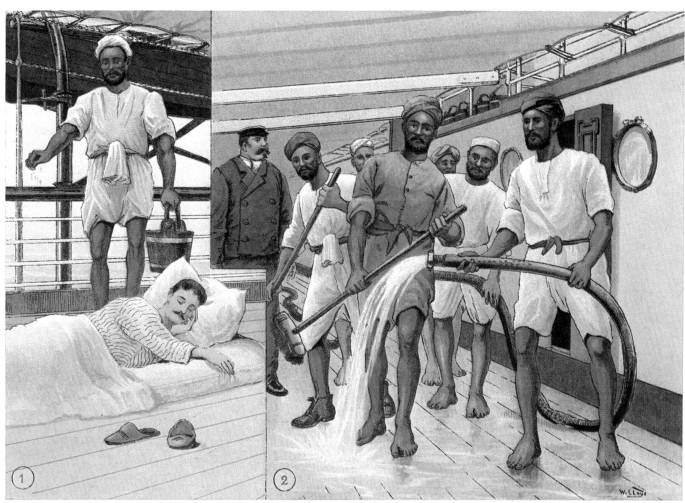

1. JACK BUSBY, JUST DROPPING OFF TO SLEEP AFTER A TROUBLED NIGHT, IS INCLINED TO BID DEFIANCE TO THE SOLITARY LASCAR WHO, ARMED WITH A BUCKET OF SAND, IS NOISELESSLY SPRINKLING THE DECK IN THE VICINITY OF JACK'S HEAD.

2. BUT IS UTTERLY ROUTED BY THE TRIBE THAT FOLLOWS ARMED WITH THE HOSE AND SCRUBBING BRUSHES, AND HE HAS TO RETIRE DEFEATED INTO THE ROASTING DECK HOUSE.

IN THE RED SEA.—THE MORNING WATCH.

OFF ADEN

1. EVENING AMUSEMENTS.—A CORNER OF THE SALOON.

2. PASSING THE P. & O. "PARAMATTA" HOMEWARD BOUND.

EVENING IN THE INDIAN OCEAN.

The Kids' tea

Professional advice.

A storm at sea

Tied in with tape
A sketch in the saloon

OUR SMALL PASSENGERS.

P. & O. PENCILLINGS.

SUNDAY MORNING MUSTER.

IN THE INDIAN OCEAN.

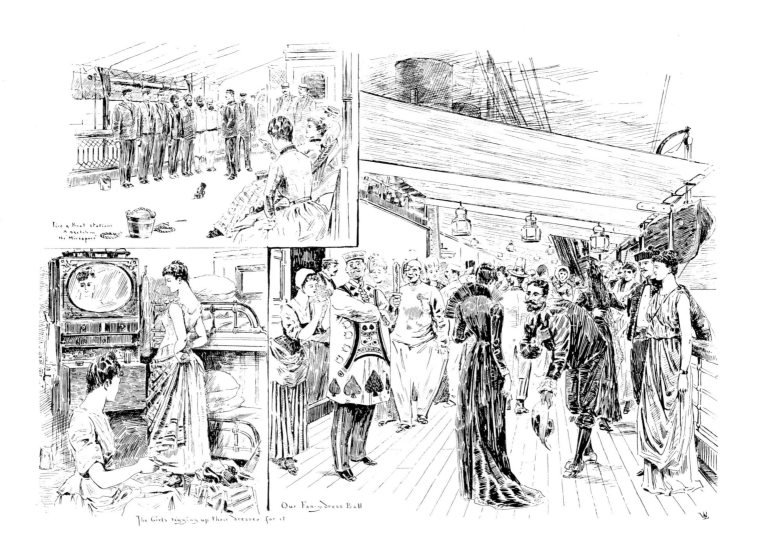

Fire & Boat stations.
A Sketch on
the Mirzapore

Our Fancy dress Ball

The Girls rigging up their dresses for it

OUR FANCY DRESS BALL.

1. THE SMOKING ROOM.

2. THE MUSIC ROOM.

FAVOURITE SPOTS.

Heaving the log.

The log ship

Thick weather.
getting a cast with the sounding machine.

NAVIGATION DUTIES.

DIVINE SERVICE IN THE SALOON.

SUNDAY MORNING.

The end, and to most people, the only sad part of the voyage
has come at last, though two of our friends, at least
have determined to stick to, the good old motto

Quis Separabit ..

Published in Great Britain by
George Weidenfeld & Nicolson Limited
91 Clapham High Street
London SW4 7TA

ISBN 0 297 79196 6

Printed in Italy